I'm OK in OK

The Diary of My Year in Oklahoma

by
Wolf von Bernuth
with
Karen Carlson-Kreibohm

W0293643

Cornelsen

I'm OK in OK
The Diary of My Year in Oklahoma

von
Wolf von Bernuth, Berlin

in Zusammenarbeit mit
Karen Carlson-Kreibohm, Berlin

Umschlag
Angelika Fischer, Berlin (oben)
Witold Skrypczak/Lonely Planet Images (unten)

www.cornelsen.de

1. Auflage, 10. Druck 2010

Alle Drucke dieser Auflage sind inhaltlich unverändert und können im Unterricht nebeneinander verwendet werden.

© 1990 Cornelsen Verlag, Berlin

Das Werk und seine Teile sind urheberrechtlich geschützt. Jede Nutzung in anderen als den gesetzlich zugelassenen Fällen bedarf der vorherigen schriftlichen Einwilligung des Verlages. Hinweis zu §§ 46, 52 a UrhG: Weder das Werk noch seine Teile dürfen ohne eine solche Einwilligung eingescannt und in ein Netzwerk eingestellt oder sonst öffentlich zugänglich gemacht werden. Dies gilt auch für Intranets von Schulen und sonstigen Bildungseinrichungen.

Druck: CS-Druck CornelsenStürtz, Berlin

ISBN 978-3-464-05329-4

Inhalt gedruckt auf säurefreiem Papier aus nachhaltiger Forstwirtschaft.

August 1

Dear Wolf,

We just found out that you are going to be our German "son" for a year. We are really excited and can hardly wait to meet you.

The exchange student organization already told us a little bit about you. We heard that you play the clarinet. John is the band director at the high school, so maybe you'd like to play in the school band. Like you, we also like sports. John plays tennis and basketball and I'm on a women's softball team and also play volleyball and a little tennis.

John is 33 and I'm 26. We don't have any children (you'll be our first!), but we know a lot of young people, and I'm sure you won't have any problems finding friends your age.

I'm sorry to say we don't know very much about your country. The only foreign country we've ever been to is Mexico, but we're looking forward to learning more about Germany from you. I had three years of German in high school, but I've forgotten most of it.

I'm sure you know that Oklahoma is right in the middle of America. I'm afraid Midwest City isn't the most exciting town in the world, but it's a nice enough place to live. It's near Oklahoma City, but we really have everything we need right here in Midwest City – a big shopping mall around the corner, John's (and your!) school, the hospital where I work (I'm a physical therapist), our church, friends, etc.

Well, you'll be seeing everything for yourself in just a few weeks! Have a good flight over and we'll see you soon!!!!

Love,

Lynne and John Davis

AUGUST 20 The captain has just announced that we are now flying over Oklahoma and will be landing in Oklahoma City in twenty minutes. So I guess this is a good time to begin my Oklahoma diary. My first impression: when I look out the airplane window, all I see is flat farmland. Not terribly interesting. How do I feel? Very tired and very dirty. It's been a long time since I've seen a bed or a shower. First the flight from Berlin to Amsterdam, then the long flight to Chicago (where I had my first chance to practice English – with some Swedish girls on the plane), then a quick subway trip into downtown Chicago and back to the airport, and now I'm finally getting closer to my new "home" in Oklahoma.

I'm a little bit nervous about meeting my American family – John and Lynne Davis (am I supposed to call them "Mom and Dad"?). I wonder if I'll like them – and if they'll like me. I was a little disappointed when I found out that they won't be at the airport to pick me up, but now I'm glad – I'll have time to get some sleep and have a shower before I meet them tomorrow. Somebody from the exchange student organization is supposed to meet me at the airport.

The captain again: "Please fasten your seatbelts and get ready for landing. Thank you for flying with us and I hope you enjoy your stay in Oklahoma."

I hope so, too!

AUGUST 21 I thought I'd sleep till noon today, but I woke up at 8:30 and just couldn't sleep anymore. I kept hearing in my head "one year" – "one year in America" – "one year away from home." It seems like such a long time ...

I stayed at the Nicholsons' house (counselors from the exchange program) until John and Lynne picked me up this afternoon. My heart started beating like crazy when I heard Mrs. Nicholson call, "They're here, Wolf!!" John and Lynne had big smiles, but they looked a little bit nervous, too. John shook my hand and Lynne gave me a little hug. It was a funny situation – a little bit like we were old friends, but we had never seen each other before.

They were both wearing jeans and T-shirts. John is a big muscular guy with blond hair. Lynne is short with dark hair, not exactly slim, but not really fat, either. They always seem to be joking around and laughing. I think we're going to get along OK. We decided I should just call them John and Lynne. They were surprised that I call my German parents Heinz and Doris.

We drove to their house in their truck, as they call it. It's a Ford Bronco II (a little bit like a jeep). Along the way, Lynne did most of the talking and explained things that we passed, but I'm afraid I didn't understand too much. As we drove into their driveway, I recognized the house numbers on their house and thought, "This is it – my American home for a whole year!"

I still have jet-lag and don't have the energy to write anymore.

AUGUST 22 Slept till 10. Unpacked all my stuff, then went out for lunch with John (skipped breakfast) to a fast-food place (a hamburger and French fried onion rings – sort of like French fries, only onions and not potatoes – not bad). You can choose what you want to have on your hamburger and because my English wasn't very good, John asked me, "Do you want cheese?" "Yes." "Lettuce?" "Yes." "Onions?" "Yes." "Pickles?" I said, "Pickles???" I must have had a funny look on my face because I was thinking of German *Pickel*. I asked, "What are pickles?" John said, "Those little round green things." Suddenly I understood and we had a good laugh when I told him what *Pickel* are in German.

John showed me around Midwest City – the shopping malls, the high school, post office, banks, etc. Most of the streets are very wide and very straight with big advertising signs and big parking lots in front of the stores. I don't think the town has a real center anywhere. The Davises' house is on a smaller street with just other houses and big lawns in front – no fences in the front and no sidewalks.

In the afternoon Lynne took me to a shopping mall. That's a big group of shops and restaurants all under one roof (everything is air-conditioned, of course) with a huge parking lot around it. She bought me a T-shirt with "Oklahoma" on it. Dinner at home (pork chops, rice, salad, cookies). At about 8 p.m. Lynne drove me over to the school where John and the school band were practicing for the next football game. John introduced me to some of the kids from band and they invited me to go out to a movie with them. We drove! The first time I'd ridden in a car driven by a sixteen-year-old kid! Sat and watched the movie while eating popcorn and drinking a Coke. I felt almost like an American. It was fun. Autumn, a very nice girl, drove me home at about 11:30 p.m.

AUGUST 23 Had to get up early this morning. John took me to school to get me enrolled. Talked to the school counselor about which classes I'd like to take. There are only six periods in a day with the same subjects every day, five days a week. I have to take American history, English and some kind of sports (I chose tennis). I decided to take French so I wouldn't be too far behind my class in Germany. Typing should be practical (and hopefully not much homework!), and then art. Everybody at school has a different schedule. You get it on a little computer card.

Then John drove me to an office where I was supposed to get an ID card. I can't do much with my German passport here and need some kind of American identification. Almost all Americans use their driver's license as an ID. The very few people who don't have a license can get an ID card which looks similar to a driver's license. Anyway, a German lady we met at the office told me it would be better to get a learner's permit than to pay seven dollars just for an ID. A learner's permit is like a driver's license, but you can only drive if there's a licensed driver over 18 on the front seat of the car with you. To get one, I just have to take a written test. I got a little booklet that I have to study before I take the test.

Had lunch with John and Bill (the other band director) at a Mexican restaurant. The food was really HOT! (That doesn't mean the temperature, it means spicy, lots of pepper!) It's a good thing American restaurants always give you a glass of ice water with your meal. John told me I'd get used to it. He said you have to kill it to be able to eat it. That means you have to cover everything with "hot sauce" to kill the real taste.

At night I watched a video – *Rambo* – with Lynne. This is the first day I've gotten a headache – not from watching the movie (although it was pretty violent), but from concentrating so hard to understand the language. I took my first aspirin.

But anyway, I'M GLAD TO BE HERE!!!

AUGUST 24 My first day of school. I had a funny feeling in my stomach, but in a way, it was easier than my first day of school after we moved to Berlin from Braunschweig three years ago. In the Berlin school, I knew that the kids already knew each other real well and had been together in the same class for some years. Here, everything was new for everybody – new teachers, new groups of kids, etc.

I was late to my first class because I couldn't figure out the system of the room numbers. The school is huge! It's only two stories high, so everything is spread out a lot. There are 1,300 kids here – all of them are either sophomores (in the 10th grade), juniors (in the 11th grade) or seniors (in the 12th grade). I'm in the 12th grade here even though I was only in the 10th in Germany.

All the classes last 55 minutes, then 5 minutes to get to the next classroom. Teachers stay in their rooms and the kids come to them. There are four classes in the morning, then 40 minutes for lunch and then two more classes in the afternoon. School's over at 2:40. At lunchtime you can either eat in the school cafeteria or drive to one of the many fast food places around here. Most of the kids come to school in cars. The student parking lot is huge!

My teachers are all pretty nice, especially my French teacher. She was born in France. She thinks that I'm the best pupil in her class and should be in a higher level, but the German teacher (I met him yesterday) told me the other French teacher was a real dragon, so I want to stay where I'm at. The German teacher is a real nice guy – he goes to Germany nearly every year. We're already good friends! He told me to say "du" to him, but I usually forget. He wants me to help him teach his German classes.

Played tennis after school. Temperature was over 100° F. (about 40° C!). Went home and drank a whole bottle of ice water. My parents called from Germany. It was good to talk to them, but also a little bit strange – like they were calling from another world. Then I helped John mow the lawn.

At night we went out to a Chinese restaurant with Lynne's parents. They are "pretty nice" as John would say. I'm meeting lots of new people every day. Everybody says, "Are you the German exchange student?" When you're new here, everybody wants to get to know you. It's great.

AUGUST 26 My first test in American history: I failed it. We all got a sheet of paper with a map of the US on it and we had to put the names of all the fifty states on the map. Impossible. But I wasn't the only one who failed it – so did 17 other kids. I think I'm going to have to work in that class!

AUGUST 28 I've been here exactly one week now, but it seems like a lot longer. We stayed with John's brother Joel this weekend. He lives on a farm near Wichita, Kansas (about four hours from here). We wanted to go waterskiing on a lake, but the weather wasn't very good, so we went to a space museum instead. The family in Kansas turns on the TV in the morning and keeps it on all day. Even if nobody's watching anything (although somebody usually is), the TV is always on. Their nearest neighbors are about four miles away, so they say there isn't much else to do. The farmhouse is really nice – a big two-story house with a lot of old pioneer stuff hanging on the walls. Joel's wife collects old kitchen tools and dishes. They raise cattle and grow wheat on their farm, but Joel says it's not enough to make a living on. He works during the week for an airline company.

AUGUST 30 It's 6:30 p.m. and I'm really tired. As usual, I stayed after school today to play tennis. Got home about 4, studied French vocabulary words (test tomorrow!) and some stuff about Columbus (test tomorrow!). Besides being tired, I've got my first sunburn and it really hurts. John wants to play tennis with me after supper, but I'd rather stay home tonight. We play either at school or at a park near here which has tennis courts that are lit at night. The courts are open to anybody – you don't have to be in a tennis club like in Germany.

SEPTEMBER 1 I went to my first football game tonight (American football, of course). The Midwest City Bombers (that's us) against the Del City Eagles (our biggest rivals – a school in the next town). Before lunch today, everybody went to the gym for a pep assembly. The idea is to get everybody excited about the game in the evening. The school band played the school song and other "fight" songs and the cheerleaders and pom-pon girls danced and jumped around and led the "cheers." Everybody shouted together in rhythm things like "WHO, WHO, WHO ARE WE? WE, WE, WE ARE THE BOMBERS, DON'T YOU SEE! GO! GO! FIGHT! FIGHT! FIGHT! WE'RE GONNA, WE'RE GONNA WIN TONIGHT!" Also at the pep assembly, some of the football players were dressed up in crazy wigs and silly dresses with lots of make-up. The one who looked the craziest was crowned "Miss Del City".

There were over 10,000 people at the game tonight! Almost all the kids from both schools plus parents, friends, people from the town, etc. The bands from Midwest City and Del City also marched around on the field before the game and at half-time. The cheerleaders in their black and gold uniforms (very short skirts) did their thing and tried to get everybody to scream and cheer. It didn't help. We lost.

SEPTEMBER 2 The police were at our school today. They came into class and took away some guys who were in a big fight after the football game last night. They probably won't be allowed to come back to school for about a month. (The school decided that, not the police.) I've heard that some years the violence after football games is even worse. One year kids from Del City broke about a hundred windows at our school.

SEPTEMBER 3 Practiced clarinet for about half an hour. I've changed my schedule and am taking band now instead of art. Anyway, I don't know why, but suddenly I started thinking about Ama. I wish I could have been able to go to her funeral to see her one last time. It's not a very nice feeling knowing that when I'm back in Germany next year, I'll never see my grandmother again. I'm glad Heinz had told me to visit her last May when I was in Braunschweig. She wanted to hear me play my clarinet so I learned two songs especially for her. Today, after I finished practicing finger exercises and marching songs for school band, I played those two songs I had learned for Ama. I was in a special mood and was thinking that maybe somehow Ama could still hear me playing those songs for her.

SEPTEMBER 4 Today we went to a lake northeast of Oklahoma City. We went waterskiing and swimming with Lynne's family. A lot of fun.

SEPTEMBER 5 My first school holiday (but just for one day). It's Labor Day today – always the first Monday in September which gives everybody a nice long weekend. Labor Day is like the First of May in Germany, except there aren't parades or demonstrations. We all slept very long today. We're going to John's parents' this afternoon for a family picnic. They live about a half-hour from here.

SEPTEMBER 8 My school routine is a little bit boring because I have the exact same six classes every day in the same order. American kids can't believe it when I tell them I had fifteen different classes in Germany. After typing, I always get cramps in my fingers, but I really want to learn that stuff. My favorite class is French. Mrs. Winfree, my teacher, always calls me "Loup." I think if the other kids in class don't remember anything else, they'll remember the French word for "wolf." Tennis isn't as good as I thought it would be. It's often very hot and so windy that the ball blows in the wrong direction.

SEPTEMBER 9 In English class today, my teacher read my essay to the class and said it was very good! That's a nice feeling. It was about Beowulf, this Old English hero who fights with monsters and dragons. It's in Old English, but we're reading a modern English translation of it.

As usual, I got home from school about 4 and had a snack.

Wrote a letter to my parents today, then did some homework and studied the little booklet for my driving test.

Went out to a Mexican restaurant for supper with John and Lynne about 6:00 as we often do when both of them are home at that time. Often one is either working or at some meeting or something at suppertime, so I eat with just one of them. A lot of times it's something from the microwave. Both John and Lynne are pretty good cooks – John makes great chili! But usually they think it's too much trouble to cook a big meal for just two or three people. We almost always watch TV during supper when we eat at home.

On an average day, I practice the clarinet for a while after supper and then do my homework – usually in the living room where John and Lynne are reading magazines and watching TV (at the same time). I go to bed at 10 or 10:30. It's a full day, but that's a good thing. I don't have so much time to think about Germany!

SEPTEMBER 10 Got two letters from home today. It wasn't very easy for me to read the part about Ama's funeral in Doris's letter. And on the last page of Heinz's letter my eyes started to get wet – but I didn't cry! I took a piece of ice and put it in my mouth. (That helps.)

SEPTEMBER 18 Another first today: my first softball game. It's almost the same as baseball, but the ball is a little bigger and softer (but not really soft if you get hit by it!). Lynne's team won, 5–2. It was fun to watch because I already knew a lot of the players, Lynne's friends. I was the score-boy and got to change the numbers on the scoreboard.

SEPTEMBER 20 During the last few days – especially at night before I go to sleep – I've always been thinking about what I would do if something happened to my mother or father or sister. It's a horrible thought, but it keeps coming into my head. At the moment, it's my biggest worry. When I think about them, I'm always telling them to be careful! I love them all so much!

SEPTEMBER 24 I understand just about everything now and have stopped carrying around my dictionary everywhere. But I do wish I could get rid of my German accent! Even if everybody says it's "cute", I don't want to sound "cute", I want to sound like an American!

SEPTEMBER 26 At our exchange program meetings in Germany before we came over here, they always told the German girls to shave their legs and under their arms. There's a German girl at our school (I don't like her very much) – and today some kids came up to me and said, "Do you know that German girl, Uschi, she doesn't shave – that looks so disgusting!"

SEPTEMBER 30 Well, the big day has arrived: I passed my driving test and got my learner's permit!!! I had studied that little booklet a lot and was sure I knew everything, but it was still pretty scary. John took me over to Del City for the test. There was a room full of little TVs on tables. First I had to fill out a form: color of eyes, color of hair, height, weight, any special illnesses, if you ever take drugs or if you drink alcohol. Then I had to go to one of the TVs and put a metal plate into the bottom of it. A picture, a question and three possible answers appeared on the screen. I had to press button A, B, or C and then right away there came a message of either "right" or "wrong". Every time the word "wrong" flashed on the screen, I got more and more nervous. I think I made three mistakes. But finally, after about twenty minutes, the words "end of test" appeared, but I still didn't know if I had passed it or not. My knees were really shaking as I went over to the desk to get the results. I passed! They took my picture and eighteen dollars and I got my license immediately. A scary feeling to think I can drive a car already just after this one test. But it also makes me feel more like a normal American and not some funny little foreigner who doesn't even know how to drive.

OCTOBER 1 It's Saturday morning. John and Lynne are at a ballgame and I'm doing my laundry. That's one of my jobs around the house along with vacuuming my own room and mowing the lawn every once in a while. Doing the laundry is really no big deal – American washing machines are a lot less complicated than German ones – just put the dirty clothes in and push a button and they're done in about a half-hour. Then stuff everything into the dryer. Even when the weather is sunny outside, they dry everything in the dryer. I don't think they even have a clothesline outside. One of the reasons I wanted to go to America was to be more independent – I guess doing my own laundry is one way of being independent, but not exactly an exciting way.

I decided to make myself a nice big breakfast this morning. Scrambled eggs, bacon, toast, cornflakes. How do I make scrambled eggs? Simple! I just take a thick glass, put two eggs into it and beat them with a fork, add salt and pepper and a little milk and then put the glass ... where? in the microwave! Set the timer for 2 3/4 minutes. After about two minutes the eggs rise higher and higher and then suddenly plop down. It's exciting to watch them! (But I'm still looking forward to good old-fashioned German-style scrambled eggs!) By the way, bacon is also cooked in the microwave. On my toast I had Oma's homemade plum jam. Wonderful!

OCTOBER 2 Another first yesterday: my first date! With a girl named Cindy. Very nice! But I'll start at the beginning.

The German teacher at school, Mr. Loveless ("Herr Lieblos" as we all call him) goes to an aerobics class at the YMCA sports center which is right around the corner from our house. I went there with him twice and then he asked me if I wanted to join. I didn't feel like spending my money for a membership, but Herr Lieblos said maybe he could find somebody who would pay it for me. A couple of days later he told me he had found someone who would love to pay for my membership: the father of one of his German students. Profession: lawyer. Money: lots. There was just one little thing ... he wanted me to take his daughter out on a date! I almost died laughing.

Anyway, Cindy is real nice and cute, too. (I don't think she has any problems getting dates, so I don't really know why her father was so interested in finding someone for her!) She had just crashed up her BMW 320 on a trip to Dallas, so her father gave her a new one: BMW 325. (Poor girl. She has the only BMW on the student parking lot.)

Last night Cindy, me, Steffen (another German guy at our school) and Joanna, Cindy's girlfriend, went out together. First we went to a restaurant (we decided beforehand that everybody would pay for their food themselves). At midnight we went to a movie – *The Rocky Horror Picture Show.* Got home at 3 a.m. – dead tired, but it was a great evening! We've already made plans to go to Dallas and New York together some day!

OCTOBER 8 Today was our Homecoming. That's a Big Day in high school life here. In the morning there was a parade through Midwest City. First in the parade was our great Marching Band (with me in it!!), then all the football players, then the Homecoming princesses riding in convertibles. The princesses wore long formal dresses – some of them were strapless, even though it was cold and drizzling outside. And then the floats. They were a little bit like our *Karnevalwagen* with big funny figures made out of paper, etc. They were built on the backs of big trucks. Different school clubs and each class (sophomores, juniors, seniors) had built a float.

Then the big football game in the evening – it's called Homecoming because former students are supposed to "come home" = come back to their old school for the game. The home team chooses an easy team to play against, so they can hopefully win the game. There was the usual band playing, cheerleaders jumping, fans screaming. During half-time, the floats and convertibles with the princesses were supposed to come out on the field, but it started raining real hard. Finished the game in the pouring rain. We lost 14–20. Nobody was in the mood to celebrate at the dance after the game. It was more or less a flop. Oh well.

OCTOBER 9 Today was the German Club picnic. We played volleyball and made hot dogs and hamburgers (typical German food!!!). Steffen and I got the keys to Joanna's car and drove around the parking lot for fifteen minutes. It was the first time I had driven an automatic.

There are about 55 members in the German Club and I am the vice-president. We meet once a month and have some kind of activity – like going to a German movie, a German restaurant or the Oktoberfest (the one in OK City, not in Munich).

OCTOBER 10 Went to church again this morning with John and Lynne. (They go every Sunday, sometimes I go with them, sometimes I don't.) There's a huge glass thing that looks like an aquarium in the front part of the church. It's a Baptist church and that's where people are baptized (not babies, but older kids or adults). Four people were baptized in the service today – two girls about my age, a boy about twelve and an older man. They all wore long white robes and went down into this "aquarium" with the pastor. He said a little prayer for each one, then one at a time they lay back and he dunked them all the way into the water and back up again.

There is always a nice friendly feeling in the church, which I like. Everybody stands around and talks before and after the service. The singing is very lively! Besides a piano and electronic organ, there's also a church orchestra that plays almost every Sunday. Lynne and John are both in it.

OCTOBER 12 I'm lying in bed with a terrible cold. I wrote three letters already today and I'll probably write a few more later. John just came in – he came home during his lunch hour to visit the "patient". He brought in a letter from my sister. Nana is home alone for two days – she probably feels like I do, alone in an empty house most of the day. It was a very nice letter. Then I read Heinz's letter again which had come yesterday. He wrote about the beautiful autumn sunshine in Germany – here it's cold and wet. I became very sad when I read the end of the letter: "I wish I could give you a little hug. Your father – who loves you very much."

OCTOBER 14 It's Heinz's birthday today and I've been thinking about Berlin all day. I hope he got the little package I sent (tennis strings – they're much cheaper here than in Germany). I thought about calling, but it's pretty expensive and we just talked on the phone together a few days ago.

OCTOBER 16 Yesterday was my first marching band contest. We went in school buses to Tulsa, about two hours from here. Along the way I talked a lot with a guy named Justin who also plays the clarinet. He's only a sophomore, but he's really smart. Like me, he also wants to be a lawyer. He doesn't know very much about Germany, but at least he asks intelligent questions – not things like whether we use toilet paper in Germany (somebody really asked me that once – they had heard we used newspaper). He knows all about economics and talks about how Japanese industry is changing the American economy, etc.

There were thousands of kids at the contest in Tulsa. All in their band uniforms, of course. Ours is a gold jacket with black trim, black pants and a black hat with a gold band. I felt really silly the first time I had to wear the band uniform – especially since the pants don't fit right and I think the whole thing is so ugly. But I guess I came over here to experience the "American way", so that's what I'm doing. In a way, I think it's fun now to wear the dumb uniform and march around in formation.

We had our first performance at 4:15. At 5 p.m. we found out we were in the finals – one of the twelve best bands! So we had to play again at 6:15. While we were getting ready, it suddenly started to rain and we saw VERY bright lightning and VERY loud thunder. We all ran behind a wall. I was worried about my clarinet getting wet. But just before it was our turn, the rain stopped again. We won fourth prize!

It was after midnight before we finally left Tulsa. Everybody was hungry, so at about 1:15 a.m. all three buses stopped at a McDonald's and 95 kids and 15 parents invaded it. Went to bed at 3:45 a.m. and slept till 11:30 this morning.

OCTOBER 21 I think the two things that people ask me about the most when they hear I'm from Germany are cars and beer. A Mercedes or BMW ("bee-emm-double-you" – or "beamer" for short) over here is almost like a Rolls Royce in Germany. People are always asking me if it's really true that you can drive as fast as you want on German highways. They're amazed about that. But they're even more amazed to hear that you have to be 18 to get a license and that it costs a lot of money to get one.

They have also heard somewhere that anybody can buy alcohol in Germany. Here you have to be 21, even to buy beer, but kids have ways of getting it anyway. Some kids drink beer on the weekends for only one reason: to get very drunk. (Not everybody, of course. I also know a lot of people – like John, for example – who never touch any alcohol at all, not even a glass of wine at special meals. Oklahoma was a dry state until 1959. That means NO alcohol at all was sold in the state – at least not legally.)

OCTOBER 25 Went to the Oktoberfest. There were about five big tents full of people – lots of them in cowboy hats and cowboy boots – drinking beer and dancing to polka music played by German bands. No, it didn't make me homesick for Germany.

OCTOBER 26 We are talking about metaphors and personification in English class. I found these nice lines from Shakespeare in my English book: "Night's candles are burnt out,/And jocund day stands tiptoe/On the misty mountain tops."

OCTOBER 27 Weather is cold and drizzly again today. I asked John to explain the difference between "drizzle" and "mist" in English. His definition: drizzle is a very light rain, but mist doesn't come straight down. When I told him that *Mist* in Germany would come straight down, we had a very good laugh.

OCTOBER 29 John liked the mist story so much, he told it to all his band students today.

OCTOBER 31 It's after midnight, but I have to write about the Haunted Houses before I forget, although I'm sure I'll never forget it! Today is Halloween, the day for ghosts and witches. There was a Halloween dance after school today. All the kids were dressed in crazy costumes and they told ghost stories. But I left early because we wanted to go to some Haunted Houses. I didn't really know what to expect. I thought it would be something like a German *Geisterbahn.* Before we left, we had some "trick-or-treaters" at the house – little kids dressed up in costumes who go from door to door and say "trick or treat" and then you put some candy in their bags. They were pretty cute.

Then off to the first Haunted House with John and Lynne and some of their friends. It was in a huge old empty factory building in Oklahoma City. We had to pay five dollars each, then walk through it in groups of five. NOTHING like a German *Geisterbahn!* It was FULL of horrible, awful, scary things. For example, one guy (real, of course) was lying on a bench and another guy dressed as a doctor was digging around in his stomach pulling out yucky things. Another guy looked like he was going to attack us with a chain saw. Everybody was screaming and holding on to each other. It was pretty awful. But fun. There are about five of these Haunted Houses in Oklahoma City. We went to two of them and Lynne really wanted to go to another one, but the rest of us had had enough, so we went back home.

NOVEMBER 3 It was cool this morning and John said he felt like a cup of hot coffee. So on the way to school at 7:30 we stopped at a drive-through fast food place and ordered two cups of coffee. John thinks it takes too long to make coffee at home in the morning.

NOVEMBER 8 Election Day today. There are lots of advertising posters around and there have been LOTS of campaign ads on TV all the time. We had an election at school yesterday just for fun and the Republicans won 728 – 310. I was surprised that some teachers even told their classes which candidates they were going to vote for. I think that would probably be illegal in Germany. John is a Republican and Lynne is a Democrat, but neither one is very interested in politics and can't really explain why they are what they are. John said he came from a family of Kansas farmers and that farmers "always" voted Republican. Lynne said good Southerners "always" voted Democrat.

NOVEMBER 11 Another football game tonight, like most Friday nights. And another pep assembly during fourth hour. Everybody has to go to them. A lot of kids would rather just get an early lunch hour, but the doors of the gym are blocked so nobody can leave early. Today five of the teachers were dressed up like the Beach Boys (only they called themselves the "Teach Boys") and sang "Surfin' USA". At another pep assembly once, some teachers dressed up like the Blues Brothers.

At the beginning of each game, the band plays the national anthem. Today I was standing on the field with the band getting ready to play and I was thinking I should feel strange being a German kid standing here playing the American national anthem. But it doesn't seem strange at all, just a normal thing to do. I still haven't really gotten used to the flag salute, though. There's a flag in every classroom and the kids have to stand up, put their right hand on their heart and say the "Pledge of Allegiance" every morning. It's part of the morning routine. After the flag salute, a member of the student council talks on the intercom (there's a loudspeaker in every classroom) and says what the lunch menu will be in the school cafeteria, the results of sports events the day before, activities of the day: club meetings, sports, assemblies, etc.

NOVEMBER 14 They announced on the intercom today that nobody was allowed to bring backpacks or schoolbags to school anymore. I thought that was the craziest thing I had every heard. They already had a rule that you weren't supposed to bring schoolbags into the classroom. They said it was too dangerous – somebody could fall over the bags on the floor. (You could bring books in a backpack, but you had to leave it in your locker and just take the books and notebooks to class.) I asked John about the crazy new rule. He said it was because they were afraid that kids would carry drugs or guns in their schoolbags.

NOVEMBER 22 My birthday! John and Lynne gave me a stuffed animal that talks and a Bomber jacket (black with "Midwest City Bombers" in big yellow letters). Went out to a German restaurant for my birthday dinner. It was supposed to look like a Black Forest restaurant, but everything was so fake. I didn't really feel at home there, but John and Lynne thought they were doing something really special for me, so I didn't want to disappoint them and say I didn't like it. The food wasn't too bad – schnitzel and sauerkraut.

At school today we had try-outs for concert band. Out of 14 clarinets, I made "second chair" (second best player)! A nice birthday present. John wants to organize clarinet lessons for me.

NOVEMBER 23 I got a funny birthday card from my sister Nana. I miss her. She had gotten the pictures I had sent of the football game and our band. She wanted to know why our school teams are called Bombers. Actually, I had never thought about it myself. I asked Justin about it. He always knows everything like that. He said it was because of the big Air Force base near here. When the high school was started in 1943, most of the kids were from Air Force families. They chose the bomber (airplane) as our school symbol.

Midwest City grew up around the Air Force base. Before the Second World War, the town didn't even exist. There were mostly potato fields and wheat fields here. But during the war, the US military was looking for a place to build an Air Force base. They wanted a place that was in the center of the country, near a big city and with plenty of flat land. Well, I can see why they picked this place. Everything is VERY flat around here: for miles and miles and miles nothing but flat land. And of course we're the center of everything here!

NOVEMBER 24 No school today and tomorrow because it's Thanksgiving. We're going to Lynne's parents' house for turkey dinner this afternoon. We already had turkey for dinner last night when John's parents came over. I'm celebrating Thanksgiving twice this year.

NOVEMBER 25 All of Lynne's brothers and sisters and their kids were at her parents' house yesterday for Thanksgiving. Same menu as the day before: turkey, mashed potatoes, gravy, mixed vegetables, salad, pumpkin pie (strange, but eatable). The men watched a football game on TV, the women talked about recipes and the kids ran around in the house.

NOVEMBER 29 Went to drama group today at church. We're working on a Christmas play and I have a part in it. The play is about a poor shoemaker in a little Bavarian village. I'm Helmut, one of the shoemaker's friends. They told me my German accent would be perfect for the play. I've been trying so hard to get rid of my accent, but now it's good for something.

NOVEMBER 30 I was the "special guest star" today in one of Mr. Loveless's German classes. The kids were supposed to interview me. The usual questions about cars and beer. Also whether we had computers and videos in Germany. I put some numbers on the board to compare Oklahoma with West Germany. Oklahoma is only a little bit smaller than West Germany, but there are only 3 million people here compared with 61 million in West Germany. The kids couldn't believe that. They asked if we still had room for farms and forests and lakes in Germany or if everything was just one huge city.

DECEMBER 1 Last night at about 10:30, I was standing in front of our house talking with John and suddenly we saw a shooting star. I think it was only the second time in my life that I had ever seen one. Right away I thought about making a wish, but I didn't think about wishing for a car or money or something like that – like I probably would have in the past. This time my wish was that Doris and Heinz and Nana would stay healthy and safe. It seemed such a natural wish at the time, that I didn't even think about it again until now.

I'm really glad my sister sent me this little Advent calendar. It's standing on the little table next to my bed. Every night before I go to bed, I'll look for the door that I can open the next morning. Tomorrow my "surprise" will be in a little boy's backpack. It's funny, now that I'm so far away from home, childish little things like Advent calendars are suddenly very important to me.

DECEMBER 3 Autumn, a girl from band, asked me today if I would be her escort. Explanation: a few days ago we elected four girls from band to be band princesses. One of them will be crowned "Miss Band" at the Christmas concert. The finalists (Autumn is one of them) choose a guy to be their escort – someone to walk across the stage with them at the concert. Anyway, Autumn asked me and I said, "Sure" in this typical "why not?" voice. On the way home I asked John about it and he said, "Yeah, that's something I wanted to talk to you about. Autumn asked me if she could ask you – and I said yes. But then I thought about it again. It would be unfair to the other guys who have been in band since 6th grade now. It's a real honor to be an escort and some guys would probably get mad because you're so new in band and are already one of the most important persons. I thought you would understand that if I explained it to you." I understood, and at least had the honor of being asked! Tomorrow I'm going to ask Autumn if she wants to go out together next weekend!

DECEMBER 5 Climbed up on the roof today and helped John put up the Christmas lights all along the outside of the house. John told me that some towns have contests to see who can decorate the outside of their house the best at Christmas time. Some people put a huge Santa Claus on their roof with a sleigh and reindeer too.

DECEMBER 6 A half an hour ago, I opened the package with the honeycake that Doris sent. I was sitting alone in the kitchen, opening the cover of the honeycake, and I felt sad. I was thinking about candlelight and Christmas music and dark rooms with just the candles shining on our Christmas tree. Just looking at that piece of honeycake in front of me reminded me of all that. Unfortunately, I couldn't share the cake with anyone – Lynne is on a diet and John is at a junior high school band concert.

The Christmas tree here is already standing in the living room, but we haven't decorated it yet. John just came back from the concert. He's wearing a gray pin-stripe suit with a white shirt and red tie. WOW! I've never seen him in a suit before. He really looks good. Lynne just asked me if I'd like to help her decorate the tree tonight – with Christmas music on the stereo. (John's going to change clothes first. He said three hours in a white shirt and tie was his limit.)

DECEMBER 7 I just wrote a Christmas letter to Heinz and Doris. I almost asked if Ama was going to go to Hamburg too to celebrate Christmas with them. That happens every once in a while – I think of Ama as a person who is still alive.

DECEMBER 8 Today was the "Hanging of the Greens" at school. Each club had made and decorated a big green wreath and members of the clubs hung them on the walls of the commons, the big open area in school. The orchestra played, the school choir sang and the principal gave a little speech. When the German Club hung up their wreath, two girls (American) sang "Silent Night" in German. I found this a bit strange.

DECEMBER 12 Today I got a letter from Heinz. Opa is dead. I still can't believe it. He was like a symbol of long life for me. Twenty minutes after I had read the letter, my sister called from Germany. I was talking English and couldn't switch into German fast enough. She didn't recognize my voice and thought I was John. I talked to Heinz and he told me Omi is living with them now. I still can't believe that I won't see Opa again when I go back to Germany. I told John about it. And then when Lynne came home, John told her about it. I was sitting in my room just staring at the envelope of Heinz's letter when Lynne came in. She felt really sorry for me and asked me if I was OK. We talked a lot about Opa and it was sad, but it made me feel good inside to talk about him and things I used to do together with him. When Lynne left she said I was a tough guy and she was proud of me. I think that helped me a lot. It's funny, when I left Germany, I knew that things would be different when I came back a year later. I knew that, but when things happen like Opa's death you realize that deep down inside there is something that doesn't want to accept any changes. It just can't be true that when I go back to Germany there won't be any Opa anymore.

DECEMBER 13 I just came home from our band's Christmas concert. There were tons of people there. The main reason was the CAR. The band bought a car (not a new one) and then we sold tickets to the concert which were also raffle tickets to win the car. We earned a lot of money selling tickets, but still not enough to pay for the car. Like a miracle, the last tickets we sold just before the concert were enough to pay for the car. But we didn't make tons of money for band trips, etc. like we had hoped to do. Oh well.

DECEMBER 16 This morning I went to school with a little bit of gray in my hair. Yesterday was the Christmas play and "Helmut" had gray hair. I thought I had gotten all the stage make-up off my face and gray stuff out of my hair, but this morning I still had make-up around my eyes and gray hair, so I went to school that way just for the fun of it. Like the day after Halloween I went to school with the black eye from the Halloween party.

DECEMBER 19 Went Christmas carolling with a group of kids from church. We rode in the church's old bus and went to about six or seven different houses and sang Christmas songs for old people. Some of them invited us in for Christmas cookies and hot chocolate or hot apple cider (like apple juice with spices). It was really nice and I like the American Christmas songs.

While riding on the bus I was talking to two girls, Jamie and Callie. We were talking about differences between the US and Germany and one of the girls asked me when Germans usually have sex for the first time. I said at about 17. Their eyes got wider and wider. They were very religious and told me they would wait until they were married. I told them I only knew one German girl who thought like that – a cousin of mine. Then they asked me how old I was. When I said "17" they went "AAHH!" They wanted to know if I had already slept with a girl. I didn't answer them.

DECEMBER 21 Last night we were sitting in the living room and Lynne was looking at the presents under the tree and shaking them (people put their presents – wrapped up, of course – under the tree about two weeks before Christmas). Then she said to John, "Don't you think we should open just one present tonight?" John laughed and said, "You try that every year! No, you'll have to wait three more days." Typical Lynne – she can't wait.

DECEMBER 22 I was supposed to play golf this morning with my history teacher, Mr. Doherty, but it's raining, so we'll go another time.

DECEMBER 23 "I was as strong as I could be – like a rock – and I stood against the wind – like a rock ..." That's the song that's playing on the radio right now and I think it describes my situation a little bit. Tomorrow is Christmas Eve!

Chris, a friend of mine who is taking German, came over this morning and asked me to help him translate a letter from Margarete Weishäuptl. Who is Margarete Weishäuptl? Some lady from Munich who wrote a letter to him in German. The last time Mr. Loveless was in Germany, he tore out some pages from the Munich telephone book. The kids in his classes picked out names and addresses. They wrote letters to people and asked them to tell them about Christmas customs in Germany. About ten kids have already gotten answers. They think it's great to get mail from Germany.

Went over to Justin's in the afternoon. Practiced clarinet for a while, then played chess, watched a movie (video) and then went out to eat with Justin and his parents. Went outside to play basketball when we got back. They have a basketball hoop and net hanging over their driveway, like most houses around here. The weather is mild and springlike now, so we won't have a white Christmas.

DECEMBER 25 I've been celebrating Christmas now for the last two days. Most people in America only celebrate on the 25th, but we had Christmas with Lynne's family yesterday and with John's family today. We went over to Lynne's parents' house yesterday along with all the grandparents, cousins, aunts and uncles. At about 5:30 we opened the presents – just one person opens a present at a time while everybody watches. Unfortunately, the kids were fighting quite a bit because they each wanted the present that somebody else got. John and Lynne say that's the part about Christmas they really hate. The TV was also on in the background – a basketball game.

We left before supper because we wanted to get to John's brother's house in Kansas before it got too late (it's a four-hour drive). While I was riding along the Oklahoma highway I couldn't help thinking about my family in Germany sitting around a table with candles and eating fish or lobster together. My Christmas Eve supper: a cheeseburger, coke and four Toffifees at a truckstop restaurant.

We got to Joel's house about 10:15 p.m. and sat under their tree (plastic) with its colorful lights (electric) and talked for a while before going to bed. This morning everybody got up when they wanted, went into the kitchen, took a paper plate and helped themselves to cinnamon rolls and cranberry bread (good!) and sat around in the living room – it didn't matter if you were still in pajamas and a robe. At about 11 in the morning we all sat around the Christmas tree, Joel read the Christmas story from the Bible and then we opened presents – again one at a time. John and I filmed everything with the video camera. John and his brother have a tradition of giving each other a lot of old junk at Christmas – broken tools, old license plates, crazy pictures, etc.

We had Christmas dinner at 2:30 – about the same as Thanksgiving with turkey and mashed potatoes and pumpkin pie. We left there about 5. My supper was another cheeseburger along the highway.

DECEMBER 26 Got a phone call from Germany today! A nice Christmas present. My sister told me that she's coming too when my parents come in May to pick me up and travel around America together. I'm really looking forward to it!

DECEMBER 28 I'm going bowling tonight with Justin and Jamie and some other kids. It's Jamie's birthday. She's 16 today. "Sweet Sixteen" as they say ...

DECEMBER 29 It's a good thing there's so much going on now during Christmas vacation: I really don't have time to think about Germany. Yesterday I went to a basketball tournament in Oklahoma City with John and Lynne. After that I went to the lock-in at the YMCA. A lock-in is where a bunch of kids are locked over night in a building and they play games and eat and talk all night long. There were about 100 kids there from the Baptist church. We had the whole YMCA to ourselves – basketball, swimming, weight room, etc. At midnight the youth pastor announced, "OK everybody, go out and get in the buses – we're going bowling." They had rented the bowling place from midnight to 3 in the morning. Then back to the Y – most people sat around and watched videos and talked till breakfast at 6:00. It was really fun! (Jamie was there, too ...) At 7 a.m. they unlocked the doors and everybody went home to get some sleep.

DECEMBER 30 Yesterday we went to Dallas. We picked up a friend of Lynne's and drove together. We spent the morning and part of the afternoon in the Galleria, a super-fancy mall in Dallas. It's about five stories high with an ice-skating rink in the middle. There was a HUGE Christmas tree in the middle covered with twinkling lights and red and gold decorations. John and I both bought a pair of shoes – the same kind, only his are size 12 and mine are size 10 1/2.

We left the mall about 4 p.m. and went to the "Supreme Court of Rock 'n' Roll" – a Hard Rock Café. It was really fantastic. A very nice café with a very nice atmosphere and very loud music. It's made to look like a courthouse with four big white pillars in front and steps leading up to the door. Inside there are long stained-glass windows with pictures of rock stars on them.

Dallas looks pretty impressive at night. There are so many skyscrapers built with lots of glass and all the lights were shining from the windows. We also saw the Reunion Tower with its huge glass ball on top that turns every hour. There's a restaurant inside it.

We got back about 10:30 and played backgammon and watched TV together. This morning when I got up Lynne told me she had persuaded John to get a puppy. It's a bichon frise: small, white, really cute. It's eight weeks old. We're going to pick it up tomorrow.

Tonight we're going to an Italian restaurant and after that to OK City to watch two basketball games – I really like basketball. John and Lynne and I have gotten a lot closer during Christmas vacation. We all know that we are going to miss each other when I go back to Germany.

JANUARY 1 Last night I was over at Jamie's house with Callie, Nancy, Justin and a bunch of other kids. There's always something going on at Jamie's. She has an older sister and a younger brother and there are always kids coming and going. It's a nice atmosphere. Everybody calls Jamie's mother "Mom". Anyway, we were watching movies and talking a lot and suddenly somebody said, "Hey, it's five after twelve. Happy New Year!" It was the first time in my life that I didn't notice when the new year arrived. We heard some cars outside honking their horns, but there aren't any fireworks or things like that on New Year's Eve.

I stayed at Jamie's till about 2 a.m. When I came home last night, the puppy was whining and yelping in the kitchen and did that all night long. It was his first night at our house. We haven't named him yet, but he's a very nice little dog. Except that he chews on my hand all the time and his teeth are like needles.

JANUARY 4 School started again today. I found out that Jamie's locker is right across from mine. I couldn't believe it! I can't understand why I never noticed her before at school. The first times I saw her at church, I didn't even know she went to my school. I must have been blind or something. How could I have missed those brown eyes and that cute little shy smile of hers?

JANUARY 6 Went with Steffen, the other German exchange student at our school, and his friends to Molly Murphy's. That's a restaurant where the waiters and waitresses always dress up in different costumes. They choose a different movie every week and dress up like the characters in that movie. This week the theme is Bugs Bunny.

After that we went to El Chico (Mexican restaurant) – not to eat again, but to pick up Tommy who works there after school and on weekends. We wanted to go to a party, but couldn't find one. While waiting for Tommy, I asked one of the girls who worked there if she knew where a party was tonight. When she said yes, all the other guys jumped up. The night was saved. I called John and Lynne to ask them what time I should be home and they told me Jamie had called to say there was a meeting at her house tonight (the youth group from church) and I could come if I wanted to. Well, it didn't take me long to make my decision. I skipped the party and the guys took me to Jamie's house.

I liked Jamie from the first moment I saw her and I soon began to love her. Sometimes when I'm in a room with her I think something is pressing on my chest and I feel like I have to run out and get some fresh air.

JANUARY 8 Went over to Jamie's after church to get the bike I left there a few days ago. She was out shopping but her mother invited me in. We talked a lot and I played with Joshua, Jamie's little brother. He's so full of energy, I can't believe it. Jamie told me he always wants me to come over and today he asked me if I could be his big brother! He's cute. I don't know how old he is, but he's just learning how to write in school.

Jamie and I got a lot closer this weekend – I'll see what's going to happen … At least I know now that she likes me, too.

JANUARY 9 I didn't hear my alarm clock this morning, but I woke up and saw a light on in the hall. It was a quarter to six. (Yawn) Time to get up. (Yawn again) I went into the bathroom and had a shower. When I came out, the house was all dark and I couldn't find John – he's usually sitting in the kitchen at that time. I looked at my alarm clock again: oh no! It was only 5:15 a.m. I had gotten up an hour too early. But I couldn't get back to sleep. I was lying on my bed – thinking about Jamie. I took out a piece of paper and began to write a poem. I didn't eat anything for breakfast, although I usually can't go to school without having eaten something. But I just wasn't hungry today. In typing class I typed the poem.

At home I had to study for semester exams – but I could hardly concentrate. Of course, it didn't help that Caspar the dog kept running all over my papers that were lying on the living room floor. For supper, I hardly ate anything and at lunchtime I hadn't felt like eating either. I finally gave up trying to study and watched an old movie on TV. But it was boring and my mind kept wandering. Then John came in and asked me to help him with his weights. (He works out with weights about three times a week.) After a while I said I was tired and was going to go to bed early tonight. He said, "You got up pretty early this morning, didn't you?" I said, "That's right – and I couldn't get to sleep last night, either." "Women" was all John said and I was really surprised. How does he know? I didn't behave differently, did I? Then we talked a lot about dating and girls. I was surprised when he told me that he had been married once before. Sometimes I can't decide if John behaves like he's my father or my big brother. I only know – that I love him! I really enjoyed our talk. Before I went to bed I took another shower to sort of get rid of everything – it helped a little bit.

JANUARY 11 Today we had semester tests during the 1st, 3rd and 5th hours and tomorrow we'll have them in the other classes. That means I had to study last night – and I did. I went over to Jamie's to study American history and she had to study for a biology test. We studied, we talked, we watched TV and we got closer and closer. I came home at about 11 p.m. – tired.

JANUARY 12 The tests weren't too bad. Mostly multiple choice ("multiple guess", as some people call it) where you just have to choose the best of four answers. If you study your notes and the material in the book – and then can remember everything – you do OK. We gave Justin a ride home from school today and we were talking about the tests. Justin said he had biology with Jamie and that the test was pretty hard. John suddenly started laughing and said, "We'll have to see what grade Jamie gets on her biology test – then we can find out if they really studied last night."

JANUARY 13 The tests are over and we've got a three-day weekend. Great! I was surprised that kids don't cheat during tests here – at least not like in Germany where we "help" each other. When I looked over the shoulder of the guy in front of me to check an answer, he immediately threw himself over his paper. I talked to Justin about it and told him about all the tricks we use in Germany, like passing answers in Kleenex packets. He was impressed! But he also said that if he took his time to study for a test, he wouldn't want to have some dumb guy steal his answers, just because he was too lazy to study himself.

JANUARY 17 We didn't have school yesterday because it was Martin Luther King Day and also the end of the semester. I was over at Jamie's for a while just doing nothing – then went to play basketball with Justin and some guys. I rode my bike as usual and people were smiling and waving when they saw me. Nobody rides a bike around here, at least not kids my age – and not in the middle of January. I like it though.

JANUARY 18 Had a potluck supper at church tonight – everybody brings either a hot-dish or a salad to share. Then we had try-outs for the next drama group play. I think I'll get a part. Afterwards the whole gang went over to Jamie's, as usual. Made popcorn, as usual. We make it in the microwave. There are lots of different flavors of popcorn – like cheese or onion. They think it's funny that we put sugar on popcorn in Germany.

JANUARY 21 Lynne and I went to Penn Square Mall this afternoon because she wanted to sign up to be on a TV game show, *Wheel of Fortune.* It's a show where you spin a wheel and have to solve a word puzzle and then you can win big prizes. There were about 2,000 people standing in line outside the mall, and probably another thousand looking for parking places. After Lynne and I waited in line for about twenty minutes, I just left the line and went up to the lady who was giving out the sign-up sheets. When I came back with the sheet, Lynne couldn't believe it. She thought we'd have to stand in line at least two hours. She filled the sheet out and we walked to the next line (only about 150 people) to hand it in. Lynne got out a postcard to write while she was waiting in line and so I just took the form, walked past the line, handed it in and came back. Nobody said anything – except Lynne, she was laughing. She asked me. "Is that the way everybody in Germany does it?"

JANUARY 27 Went over to Jamie's after school today to help her paint some shelves in her little brother's room. She loves to do things like that. When we finished, we celebrated by having some cherry cheese pie which Jamie had made herself. (Her specialty! Wonderful!)

FEBRUARY 4 Lynne is always trying to lose weight. There's been a wrapped present sitting on top of the refrigerator ever since I got here. It's for her from John, but she wasn't supposed to open it until she lost twenty-five pounds. Today she said she has lost ten pounds and she can't wait any longer. She HAS to open that present. So she did. It was a stuffed cat that you can stick on the car window – she had been wanting one. Now she says she FOR SURE is going to lose another ten pounds before my parents come over. She doesn't want them to see her fat.

FEBRUARY 10 Everybody is talking about Valentine's Day which is coming next Tuesday. I remember reading it on the calendar in Germany, but it was never a big deal. Here it is, as lots of people have told me. You give flowers or candy to your girlfriend and take her out to a movie. People send cards to all their friends. It's the biggest day of the year for flower shops in the US. So, Nancy and I went to a flower shop after school to get some flowers for Jamie. Nancy bought a rose for Mike, her boyfriend, and I bought a dozen roses for Jamie (for only $15.00 – a special deal they had that day). I didn't want to wait till Valentine's Day to give them to Jamie, so I just stopped by her house, put them in the kitchen, told Jamie's mom they were for Jamie from me for Valentine's Day, and then I left. Jamie was in her room and hadn't seen or heard me. After I left, her mom asked her to come into the kitchen. At first she didn't notice anything. Then her mom asked her to hand her a bowl that was standing next to the roses. After a minute Jamie asked her mom, "Who gave you those roses?" Her mom said, "You little dummie, they aren't for me." Jamie's mom told me later that Jamie went crazy and screamed and jumped around.

FEBRUARY 12 Jamie must have told all her friends about the roses. In church today, all the girls came up to me and said, "Oh, Wolf, you're so sweet ..." And the guys came up to me and said, "Hey, wow, Jamie is going crazy. What did you pay for those roses?" I didn't tell anybody. Later I told John the price. He told me I was really lucky. Usually you have to pay about $40 for a dozen roses. Now I know why everybody was asking me about them. People only get flowers on special days in America. They are much more expensive than in Germany.

FEBRUARY 14 Today, Valentine's Day, is the first time I've ever seen flowers in Jamie's house (besides the ones from me, that is). Jamie's mom said to me, "Wolf, I want to thank you for the flowers – a dozen red roses." I said, "Uh, I didn't send you any flowers." She said, "I know, but if you hadn't given Jamie a dozen flowers, Paul never would have given me any – so, thanks!" And she laughed, but she was serious, too. Jamie went to choir practice at church at 4:45. I talked to "Mom" and Paul, Jamie's stepfather, in the kitchen for a while and we had supper together. I went into Jamie's room and saw two envelopes lying on her bed – both of them had "For Wolf" on them – in one there was a poem and in the other some pictures of her that I had been asking for.

FEBRUARY 15 Lynne gave John a big box of chocolates yesterday for Valentine's Day and I'm helping him eat them. She promised him she wouldn't steal any of them because she is really serious about her diet now. John says he's heard that before.

FEBRUARY 18 Lynne is really excited. The people from the TV quiz show invited her (and about a hundred other people) to come for an interview. On the show, everybody screams like crazy and jumps around when they spin the wheel. That's not really the way Lynne is, but she said she did it at the interview. Now she's waiting to hear if she'll be a candidate on the show and get to go to California to the studio.

FEBRUARY 24 Went on a choir trip to Tulsa this weekend. We stayed in a fancy hotel next to a mall. At night we played with the room telephones and made crazy phone calls to kids from our group who were in other rooms. We sat around on the huge beds and drank apple juice out of champagne glasses and watched MTV (rock videos) and felt like kings. Oh yes, we also did some singing with a bunch of different choirs.

Tulsa is supposed to be the oil center of the world. Most of the big oil companies have huge office buildings downtown. There are oil wells all over the place. There are a lot in Oklahoma City, too, but not as many as in Tulsa. (In Oklahoma City there are even oil wells on the lawn right next to the State Capitol building.)

MARCH 4 Lynne's disappointed because she heard today she wasn't selected to be on the TV show. So she said she needs to have a big bowl of banana-nut ice-cream with chocolate sauce (her specialty) to make her feel better. She says her diet can wait till tomorrow.

MARCH 6 We had a lot of snow this weekend. Almost all the schools in Oklahoma are closed – except ours! Only about 47% attendance in school today, so they really should have closed it. I can't remember any time in Germany when schools were closed because of bad weather. I told John about our *Hitzefrei* in Germany and he thought it was really funny. "What! No school when it's only 78 degrees. Hey, now that's a good idea you Germans have!"

MARCH 13 The snow is gone, but now it's very windy and stormy. I got a letter from Boris today with all the news from my school in Berlin. He said they couldn't believe that I only had six classes and that I didn't even have to take math!

Boris wrote that they hadn't had history or biology for a while because the teachers were sick. I hadn't thought about it before, but I don't think any classes here in Oklahoma have ever been canceled because a teacher was sick. Sometimes there's a substitute who teaches the class, but it's an extra teacher who just comes to substitute, not one of the regular teachers. I asked John if he could remember if a class had ever been canceled and he said no. He thinks there's probably some state law about it.

MARCH 14 I've just experienced the first duststorm of my life. Wow! We were at a tennis tournament in Shawnee when it suddenly got VERY windy and then we saw this gray-brown wall of dust moving towards us. It was really frightening. Even though it was only 4 p.m. and there were no clouds in the sky, the dust blocked out the sun and it was dark. Dust was in EVERYTHING – our hair, our eyes, between our teeth. I couldn't believe it. We had seen a movie in school a few weeks ago about the duststorms of the '30s. Now I can imagine how those people then must have felt. A lot of them left Oklahoma and headed for California – like the family in Steinbeck's *Grapes of Wrath*.

MARCH 23 It's 3 p.m. but I'm having breakfast now because I just got up. I've been on a ski trip in Colorado and we didn't get home until 7 this morning (it's a sixteen-hour drive). I went with a group of international students. It was a nice feeling to be able to communicate with these kids from France, Spain, Japan, Italy, etc. – all in English.

The snow was great except for the time I was almost buried alive when I lost my skis in deep fresh snow. This Italian guy, Julio, and I wanted to try a great-looking slope even though there was a sign saying "Slope Closed". It took me about 15 minutes to find my skis and get out of the deep snow. I called out to Julio that I was OK. I found out later that he was already over another hill and hadn't heard me. So if I hadn't been OK, nobody would have heard me. That scared me a little!

Another day we rented a snowboard. That's like a skateboard only longer and your feet are fastened to it. It's very difficult. We spent most of the time sitting in the snow.

We went to Colorado in seven vans and all the vans had CB radios. We talked and sang on the radio to the kids in the other vans while we were driving along the highway. A French teacher had brought a bottle of wine along which we passed around. At the exchange program meetings they had always told us to be VERY careful with alcohol and that it was illegal to have any open bottles of alcohol in a car. But nobody seemed to care. Three of the vans also had fuzz-busters. Whenever our fuzzbuster started giving a signal, Mr. Leslie would get on the CB and tell all the other vans, "We've got a 'red alert' here – remember, speed limit here is five five." (55 miles per hour).

MARCH 26 It's Easter. After church today I went over to the mall to get a haircut and noticed that there were plastic eggs lying all over the place and lots of little kids with baskets. Actually, I hadn't really thought much about it being Easter until I saw all the eggs. I went over to Jamie's house in the afternoon and all her little cousins were there. They had fun looking for Easter eggs in their backyard. I also got a little basket with seven chocolate eggs from Jamie's family.

MARCH 30 I went to Indian City, USA today with a bunch of junior high kids. A friend of Lynne's who teaches 7th grade history invited me to go along on the school bus with her class. Indian City is like an outdoor museum with all different kinds of Indian houses. We had an Indian guide who explained everything to us. I didn't know that Oklahoma used to be Indian Territory. Indians from other parts of America who were forced off their old homelands had to come and live here. Some of them had to walk thousands of miles to get here and a lot of them died along the way. The Indians called the trip to Oklahoma the "Trail of Tears".

There are a lot of souvenir shops in Indian City where Indians sell hand-made things to tourists. I bought some nice jewelry for Jamie and Nana.

APRIL 1 This morning John and I went to Norman (about 20 minutes away) to buy shoes at a tent sale. They put up a big tent on a parking lot and sell cheap shoes there. On the way up there I saw a funny-looking animal (dead) lying on the road. It was about as big as a cat, but it wasn't a cat. John told me it was a raccoon. He said they hunt raccoons in the South and in parts of the Midwest and some people eat them. I thought maybe that was an April Fool's joke, but he said he was serious. They hunt them by blinding them with a bright light and when the raccoon can't see, it stands still and then the hunter shoots it.

Another dead animal that I've seen (rather: smelled!) around here on the highway quite often is a skunk. They really stink. I couldn't believe it the first time I smelled one.

APRIL 9 John and Lynne had a garage sale today. That's a little bit like a flea market, but in your own garage. You put all the old stuff you don't want anymore in your garage or on the front lawn and wait for people to come and buy it. John and Lynne had a little ad in the local paper and they also put up a sign down on Reno, the main street, saying "GARAGE SALE TODAY" and an arrow pointing to our street.

John wasn't a very good salesman. A lady picked up an old lamp and asked, "Does this lamp work OK?" Greg, John's friend who was helping at the sale, said, "Yes, ma'am, it only needs a new light bulb and it will be just like new." John laughed and said, "Although I doubt if you'll be able to find another bulb that fits." Lynne kept getting madder and madder at John because he was just making a joke out of everything and didn't seem interested in selling the junk.

They started the sale at 8:00 a.m., but they were afraid the first people would come around 7 to get a look at the "good stuff". Lynne told me there are "professional" garage sale lookers who spend every weekend cruising garage sales looking for bargains for themselves or for stuff they can sell again and make money with. Anyway, the night before the sale, Lynne put up a sign on the door for any early-birds: "Please don't ring the doorbell – child is sleeping." That child was me.

APRIL 10 I watched Jamie's team practice softball this afternoon. Then went over to her house and we did our homework together. Also played with Josh, her little brother, for a while. His favorite toys are star wars things and a G.I. Joe doll (like a Barbie doll, only it's an army soldier). He also watches a lot of violent stuff on TV.

APRIL 14 We had a band contest in Putnam City today. We went up there in school buses. Then we went to Haribear's to eat. Our table was pretty big – we were about twelve people. Somebody asked me a question about Berlin, where it was located. I didn't have any paper to draw a map, so I took two plates and put them next to each other – one for West Germany, one for East Germany. Then I took a little packet of sugar, tore it in half and put both halves of the sugar packet paper next to each other on the "East Germany" plate. That was East and West Berlin. I built the Berlin Wall around West Berlin out of sugar. Slowly all the countries in Europe appeared on the table in the form of glasses, forks, sugar packets, plates, etc. Whenever someone named a country in Europe, I added it to our "map". Russia was a red ketchup bottle, Iceland was a glass of ice-water, etc.

Then I started playing teacher and asking them questions: "Where is Italy? – Right! It's the fork ..." We had a good time.

Gene was eating his onion rings and suddenly asked, "Wolf, could you hand me Russia, please?" Then I asked Tracy, "Where is Iceland?" Tracy: "In Gene's hand." I looked over to Gene. She was right. He had just drunk Iceland.

APRIL 18 Today my history teacher told me that some kids had said to him they had learned more in a half-hour at Haribear's than during seven months in his class – and I really believe they did. Mr. Doherty asked me if I could explain the map of Europe with ketchup and democratic/communistic plates in one of his classes. I'm not sure if he was kidding or not.

APRIL 19 Two things I noticed in school today: one – most kids do all their assignments and tests in pencil. The only time you have to use ink (and then only ball point – I've never seen anybody write with a fountain pen over here) is sometimes for special essays or for term papers. Term papers are long reports (about 20 pages or more). The teachers want us to type them if at all possible.

Two – Mr. Shakleford, the guidance counselor, can make his tie jump up and down by moving his Adam's apple.

APRIL 20 Today John and Lynne took me to the Arts Festival in Oklahoma City. It was great. The artists had their drawings and photographs and paintings set up on tables outdoors. I realized I hadn't been to something "cultural" like that in the eight months I've been in Oklahoma. I didn't know I missed it so much.

I noticed that a lot of the artists had German last names – their grandparents or greatgrandparents had probably come from Germany. It made me feel good to know that there's a part of me that belongs to that German cultural world, too.

APRIL 21 Today we had a "Quiz Bowl" at school. Everybody went to the auditorium for two hours to watch the three teams compete against each other – a sophomore, a junior and a senior team – with six kids on each team. First the sophomores competed against the juniors, then the winner (juniors) against the seniors. The seniors in the audience were really upset when the "little" juniors beat them. Everybody cheered for their class's team almost like at a football game! There were questions about math, history, geography, science, art and music. The kids on the teams had buzzers at their tables and whoever pushed the buzzer first got to answer the question (or try to answer it). Some of the kids on the teams were chosen by other kids and some were chosen by teachers. I couldn't believe how smart they were! It was fun and exciting to watch because I knew most of the kids competing.

APRIL 22 John and Lynne went with John's brother and his wife to Guthrie today for the Oklahoma Centennial Festival. (I didn't feel like going and besides, there was a drama group rehearsal today.) At 12 o'clock noon exactly one hundred years ago today, over 50,000 people on horseback and in wagons pulled by horses or oxen stampeded into central Oklahoma to get a piece of the land. (Before that, Oklahoma was Indian Territory. At first Oklahoma was supposed to be only for Indians, but then the palefaces decided they needed more land.) Towns like Guthrie (the first capital) and Oklahoma City were started on that day – as big groups of tents. Some of the people couldn't wait till noon and went – illegally – into the territory sooner than the others. They were called "Sooners" and that's why Oklahoma is called the "Sooner State". The famous university football team from Oklahoma is also called the "Sooners". Anyway, so much for Oklahoma history.

John thought the parade was pretty boring, just an endless stream of horses and old wagons and people dressed in pioneer costumes. His brother Joel loved it, though. He loves to look at horses and cattle. There was also a big fireworks show in the evening.

APRIL 30 Tonight at 10:30 John wanted to take his truck over to a place that would repair it in the morning. Why at 10:30 p.m.? Well, Lynne was in San Diego, so he wanted me to help him. He wanted me to drive the truck over there and he would drive their other car so we would have it to come home in. Of course, I don't have a real license (just a learner's permit), so what we did was illegal.

Fortunately, everything went fine. I followed behind John and started smiling when I looked at the speedometer and saw that he was going over the speed limit. A good reason for any policeman to stop us. I just turned up the radio and followed along at the same speed ... Jamie's mom knew we were planning to do this. She was worried that she would have to visit me in jail the next day. She said, "Whenever you and John are alone, I just know you're going to do crazy stuff. But I also know that I can't do anything to stop you guys."

MAY 12 Brady, a guy in my typing class, and I have been ditching the last twenty minutes of class regularly now for the past two or three months. Whenever we finish our assignments, we ask the teacher for a hall pass to go to the library to study. (You aren't allowed to be out in the halls without a little yellow paper signed by a teacher saying where you are going.) We almost never went to the library with this pass, but instead we left school in Brady's car and usually went to a Mexican restaurant for lunch. Well, yesterday was the first time that our typing teacher checked on us in the library – and naturally we weren't there. But he couldn't prove that we had left school. We said we were just out in the halls somewhere. If he found out that we had left school, Brady and I would have gotten an "in-house". That's when you have to spend the whole day studying in a special room with only three short breaks. You can also get an in-house for being rude to a teacher or for saying a "bad" word in class. I did that once a few months ago. (I thought it was a very harmless little word – we say it all the time in Germany – but the teacher asked me to stay after class. He told me if I said it again, I'd get an in-house.)

MAY 13 Tonight is the band banquet. John said there was a hypnotist there last year and he's coming again tonight. Last year he told a black guy he was Michael Jackson and suddenly the guy started singing, dancing and talking like Michael Jackson. Then the hypnotist told five people that they were watching a horse race and they had to cheer for their horse to win. Everybody's horse won and everybody got $50,000. Then the hypnotist told everybody that the person next to them had stolen their money. The reactions were really funny.

MAY 14 Last night was super: – a chicken dinner, the hypnotist, some songs and speeches and the presentation of awards (I got one, too!). Jamie and I got back to her house at about midnight.

Came home from Jamie's at about 11:45 a.m. this morning.

Today is Mother's Day. I gave a card and a rose to Lynne and a card to Jamie's mom. Lynne was very happy and Jamie's mom told me later that she had cried when she read my card. We had lunch with John's parents. Then I had to go to rehearsal. Today was the big day! – Our drama performance! We were great, as usual. After the play, Mike and Nancy and Jamie and I went to the ice-cream store –

with our stage make-up on. (The girls always put our stage make-up on for us before the play – Jamie was my make-up girl – nice!) All the people in the ice-cream place stared at Mike and me and gave us funny looks. We just about died laughing.

MAY 17 John and Lynne are starting to work like crazy in the house. Lynne is wallpapering the hallway. John is putting in a new front door. I'm supposed to paint my room. Lynne bought flowers for the front yard and planted them. All this is because my parents are coming soon and they want everything perfect.

MAY 18 I got my driver's license today! The real one, this time. I was supposed to take the test yesterday, but it was drizzling and they don't give the test when the roads are wet. On the way over there, John suddenly said, "Hey Wolf, do you know how to parallel park? I think they'll ask you to do that." I didn't know what he was he talking about, so we stopped at a parking lot along the way and practiced. The test itself was pretty easy. I took it in John's truck (you have to bring your own car). I'm afraid I still have a foreign accent, so the guy who was testing me asked where I was from. When I said Germany, he said, "Oh really! I was in Germany for three years with the Army. I loved it." And then he spent the whole time telling me about all the places he had been to in Germany. He didn't really pay much attention to my driving. I had to parallel park, too, and I wasn't too good at it, but he said it was good enough. I passed!

MAY 19 Tonight is the prom. I'm sitting in fifth hour and none of the girls are working (neither am I). The girls are telling each other what color their dresses are, where they're going out for dinner, what car they'll be driving in (lots of guys rent fancy cars, even limousines!) and of course, the most important thing – WHO they're going with. Some girls even left after fourth hour today to go home and get ready (it doesn't start until 8:00 p.m.). The girls are all going crazy about it! Jessica just told me: first you go out for dinner to a fancy restaurant, then you go to the prom (it's at the ballroom of some university). Everybody spends tons of money on clothes. Some of the guys rent tuxedos. The prom is a dance with refreshments, but Jessica said most people don't dance very much, but spend most of their time standing around waiting to have their pictures taken. Professional photographers take pictures of each couple in front of an artificial background. According to Jessica, the pictures are the most important part of the prom.

Jamie thinks it's pretty crazy and a big waste of money. We're going to go to a movie together tonight instead. And some of the money we save by not going to the prom we can spend in Dallas tomorrow.

MAY 20 Went to Dallas today with John and Lynne and Jamie. John let me drive on the highway for almost two hours. We had lunch at the Hard Rock Café and then Jamie and I spent the rest of the day at Six Flags over Texas, one of the biggest amusement parks in the US. It's called that because during its history, Texas has been under six different flags: Spanish, French, Mexican, Republic of Texas, the Confederate States and the US. Different parts of the park have buildings and costumes typical to the six different times. But the main thing about the park is, of course, the rides. The only time I had been on a roller coaster before was when I was seven years old and I got sick on it. This time I loved it! Even though we sometimes had to wait in line for over an hour. It was awfully hot and humid. On the way back to Midwest City, both of us fell asleep in the back seat of John's truck.

MAY 22 Jamie and I finished painting my room today. Everything is supposed to look good for my parents and sister. Jamie and I both know that we only have five more days together – but for some reason, neither of us talks about it.

MAY 23 My parents and sister arrive tomorrow! Lynne is going crazy – cleaning the house, washing windows, baking a cake. She's so worried that my mother won't like her and that she'll think she wasn't a good enough mother for me this year. I keep telling her everything was just fine, but she's worried anyway. John says he can't wait to meet my dad.

MAY 24 They're here! Doris, Heinz and Nana arrived this afternoon. John, Lynne, Jamie and I were all at the airport to meet them. I had a funny feeling in my stomach while we were waiting for them to come. Suddenly, there they were and everybody was shaking hands and hugging each other and laughing. I was wearing my stage make-up because there was a drama group performance this evening. They looked at my make-up and John told Nana, "Your brother always goes around like this now. It's an old American custom." She didn't understand him so I had to translate. My mother said later that she had been a little bit worried at first. She thought, well, a lot can happen in a year. Maybe he's changed. I explained about the performance and they all laughed.

We went to the performance together tonight (I think they liked it), had sandwiches back here at John and Lynne's and now they've gone back to their motel for the night. Tonight during the performance I felt happy and sad at the same time – happy that my family was here but sad because it was my last time to be with the drama group.

MAY 25 Graduation Day. The Big Day for 440 seniors at Midwest City High School. We all wore long black robes and funny black hats with gold tassles on top. As the school orchestra played a slow march by Elgar, we all marched into the gymnasium. We sat in rows of chairs set up on the basketball courts and our parents sat along the sides. The principal and some lady from the University of Oklahoma gave speeches and all the seniors sang the school song together: "May memories of our high school go with us through life, and be an inspiration to aid us in our strife. Bomber pride, grow inside, may we ere be bold. Loyal to our true colors, the glorious black and gold."

The school choir sang "One Moment in Time". Two girls did the hand motions to it in deaf sign language. I don't think there were any deaf people there, it was more symbolic, but it was really nice.

Then the big moment when they called off the names of all 440 seniors. We walked to the front, shook some hands, took our diplomas from the principal and then flipped our tassles to the other side of our caps. At the end of the ceremony, we all threw our caps up into the air.

A lot of kids went to parties afterwards. For me, the nicest way to celebrate was at my favorite Mexican restaurant with all my favorite people: John, Lynne, Doris, Heinz, Nana and Jamie.

MAY 26 We had already shown my parents everything there is to see in Midwest City yesterday, so today we just sat around and talked most of the morning. We walked around for a while at the mall and had lunch there. After lunch, I took a walk around the neighborhood with Doris and Nana. My mother said to me, "And now what are we going to do, Wolf? There really doesn't seem to be much to do around here." I suppose she's right. There aren't many tourists who come here, especially not from Europe. But in all the nine months I've been here, I don't think I ever thought of this place as boring. If you know a lot of people here, like I do, there's always something to do.

Well, John thought of something for us to do. We went to a horse race at Remington Park. My dad especially enjoyed that. He liked to watch John and Lynne bet on the horses. John was so excited when his horse won something. He kept saying "Big Money! Big Money!" and was expecting to make a lot of money. My dad had to laugh when John found out how much money he had won: five dollars.

MAY 27 John is so impressed with the idea that we can trace our family back over two hundred years. He thinks somebody in his family came from Ireland and somebody from England, but he doesn't know when they came or anything about them.

We all went to a baseball game today (Nana thought it was boring) and then to a nice restaurant for a steak dinner (very good). At dinner my parents were talking to John and Lynne about the advantages and disadvantages of having children. Of course, Nana and I were sitting there listening, so they couldn't say too many negative things. Lynne said, "You don't have to talk me into it. I'd love to have a baby. It's John you have to convince." John doesn't want to have kids because he's afraid of losing his independence.

Well, this is my last night in Midwest City. I'm sitting here on my bed looking at my suitcases that are standing by the door. "All my bags are packed, I'm ready to go ..." I keep hearing in my head that old song from the '60s. "Don't know when I'll be back again ..."

But I know it will be soon.

MAY 28 We're on our way to California. I'm sitting in a rented car with Doris and Heinz and Nana. Before we left today, after the car was all packed and my parents and sister were in the car ready to go, John and Lynne and I went back into the house and went into my room for one last time. We had promised each other there wouldn't be any tears, but it wasn't easy. We said good-bye and then John said, "Wolf, there's something we want to give you ..." And he gave me the keys to their house and their cars. I've got them in my pocket and I keep playing with them as we drive along the highway.

We just drove past a sign: "YOU ARE NOW LEAVING OKLAHOMA. PLEASE COME AGAIN!"

I will.

June 25

Dear Wolf,

By the time you get this you'll be back home again after your trip to the West Coast. Hope you had a good time together with your parents and Nana.

It was a great year with you, Wolf, and we both want to thank you for staying with us. We had so much fun together and shared so many happy – and sometimes sad – times together. The house is really empty without you.

But ... not for long. Guess what!!! Yes, we're going to have a baby. He or she (John is sure it's going to be a boy!) will have "your" room. Don't worry, though, we'll always find room for you when you come to visit us again – hopefully very soon.

I'll write more in a few days and give you all the other news from Midwest City. Give our love to Heinz and Doris and Nana. It was so good to meet them all. They're wonderful people!

Lots and lots of love from your
American family,

Lynne, John and ???

Vocabulary

AE = American English, *BE* = British English, *infml.* = informal, *pl.* = plural, *sb.* = somebody, *sth.* = somethin

A **actually** ['æktʃʊəlɪ] eigentlich
ad [æd] Anzeige, Werbung
advertising ['ædvətaɪzɪŋ] Reklame
(to) **aid** [eɪd] helfen
Air Force ['eə fɔːs] Luftwaffe
alarm clock [ə'lɑːm klɒk] Wecker
alert [ə'lɜːt] Alarm
amusement park [ə'mjuːzmənt pɑːk] Vergnügungspark
(to) **announce** [ə'naʊns] ankündigen, durchsagen
arrow ['ærəʊ] Pfeil
artificial [ɑːtɪ'fɪʃl] künstlich
assignment [ə'saɪnmənt] *AE:* Schulaufgabe
attendance [ə'tendəns] Anwesenheit
audience ['ɔːdjəns] Zuschauer
average ['ævərɪdʒ] durchschnittlich
award [ə'wɔːd] Auszeichnung, Preis
awful ['ɔːfʊl] schrecklich

B **backpack** ['bækpæk] Rucksack
banquet ['bæŋkwɪt] Festessen
(to) **baptize** [bæp'taɪz] taufen
bargain ['bɑːgɪn] günstiges Angebot
base [beɪs] Stützpunkt
bench [bentʃ] Bank
besides [bɪ'saɪdz] außer
(to) **bet** [bet] wetten
bichon frise ['biːʃɔːn friː'zeɪ] *Hundeart*
bold [bəʊld] tapfer, kühn

bottom ['bɒtəm] Unterteil
bowl [bəʊl] Schüssel
bunch [bʌntʃ] Gruppe
button ['bʌtn] Knopf
buzzer ['bʌzə] Piepser
by doing sth. indem/dadurch, daß man etwas macht

C **cafeteria** [kæfɪ'tɪərɪə] Mensa, Speisesaal
campaign [kæm'peɪn] Wahlkampf
(to) **cancel** ['kænsl] ausfallen lassen
candle ['kændl] Kerze
candy *(sing.)* ['kændɪ] *AE:* Süßigkeiten
cap [kæp] Mütze
CB radio (CB = Citizens' Band**)** *Privatfunk*
centennial [sen'tenjəl] Hundertjahrfeier
(to) **cheat** [tʃi:t] mogeln
cherry ['tʃerɪ] Kirsche
chest [tʃest] Brust
chili *(AE)* = chilli *(BE)* ['tʃɪlɪ] *mexikanischer Bohneneintopf*
cinnamon ['sɪnəmən] Zimt
Confederate States [kən'fedəreɪt] *die Südstaaten im amerikanischen Bürgerkrieg*
contest ['kɒntest] Wettbewerb
convertible [kən'vɜ:təbl] Kabriolett
cookie (*AE*) ['kʊkɪ] Keks
council ['kaʊnsl] Rat
couple ['kʌpl] Paar
courthouse *(AE)* Gerichtsgebäude
cranberry ['krænbərɪ] Preiselbeere
cute [kju:t] niedlich

D **date** [deɪt] Verabredung
(to) **date** [deɪt] mit jm. ausgehen
deal [di:l] Sache, Angelegenheit

(to) **decorate** ['dekəreɪt] schmücken
(to) **dig** [dɪg] wühlen
disgusting [dɪs'gʌstɪŋ] widerlich
(to) **ditch** [dɪtʃ] schwänzen
(to) **doubt** [daʊt] bezweifeln
dozen ['dʌzn] Dutzend
driveway *(AE)* Einfahrt
drizzle ['drɪzl] Sprühregen
(to) **drizzle** ['drɪzl] nieseln
drunk [drʌŋk] betrunken
dumb [dʌm] dumm, doof
(to) **dunk** [dʌŋk] tauchen
duststorm Staubsturm

E **eagle** ['i:gl] Adler
(to) **enroll** [ɪn'rəʊl] einschreiben, anmelden
ere *(poetisch)* [eə] immer
escort ['eskɔ:t] Begleiter/in
(to) **experience sth**. [ɪk'spɪərɪəns] etwas erleben, etwas kennenlernen

F **fake** [feɪk] künstlich
fancy ['fænsɪ] schick, ausgefallen
(to) **fasten** ['fɑ:sn] befestigen
(to) **figure out** begreifen
(to) **flash** [flæʃ] aufleuchten
flavor *(AE)* = flavour *(BE)* ['fleɪvə] Geschmack
flea [fli:] Floh
float [fləʊt] Festwagen
former ['fɔ:mə] ehemalig
fortune ['fɔ:tʃu:n] Glück
fountain pen ['faʊntɪn pen] Füllfederhalter
frightening ['fraɪtnɪŋ] beängstigend
funeral ['fju:nərəl] Beerdigung
fuzzbuster *(AE)* ['fʌzbʌstə] Radardetektor

G (to) **get used to sth.** sich an etwas gewöhnen
G.I. *(infml.)* US-Soldat
gonna *(infml.)* ['gɒnə] = going to
gotten *(AE)* ['gɒtn] *Partizip Perfekt von* (to) get
graduation [grædʒʊ'eɪʃn] *AE:* Schulabschlußfeier
gravy ['greɪvɪ] (Braten-)Sauce
(to) **guess** [ges] *AE:* glauben, meinen

H **half-hour** = half an hour
Halloween [hæləʊ'i:n] *die Nacht vor Allerheiligen*
Hard Rock Café *Name einer Kette von Musiklokalen*
haunted ['hɔ:ntɪd] Spuk-
height [haɪt] Größe
highway *(AE)* ['haɪweɪ] Autobahn
honeycake ['hʌnɪkeɪk] Honigkuchen
(to) **honk** [hɒŋk] hupen
honor *(AE)* = honour *(BE)* ['ɒnə] Ehre
hoop [hu:p] Reifen
horrible ['hɒrəbl] schrecklich
hug [hʌg] Umarmung
(to) **hug** [hʌg] umarmen
humid ['hju:mɪd] feucht

I **immediately** [ɪ'mi:djətlɪ] sofort
ink [ɪŋk] Tinte
intercom ['ɪntəkɒm] Lautsprecheranlage
(to) **invade** [ɪn'veɪd] überfallen

J **jet-lag** ['dʒet læg] *Schwierigkeiten durch Zeitumstellung*
jocund *(poetisch)* ['dʒɒkənd] heiter, frohsinnig
(to) **join** [dʒɔɪn] Mitglied werden
junk [dʒʌŋk] Kram
just: We just found out. *(AE)* = We have just found out. *(BE)*

K (to) **kid** [kɪd] Jux machen

L **labor** *(AE)* = labour *(BE)* ['leɪbə] Arbeit
laundry ['lɔːndrɪ] Wäsche
lawn [lɔːn] Rasen
lettuce ['letɪs] Kopfsalat
level ['levl] Niveau
license plate *(AE)* = licence plate *(BE)* ['laɪsəns pleɪt] Nummernschild
lightning ['laɪtnɪŋ] Blitz
line [laɪn] Schlange
lit [lɪt] beleuchtet
lobster ['lɒbstə] Hummer
located [ləʊ'keɪtɪd] gelegen
locker ['lɒkə] Schließfach

M **ma'am** [mæm] (= madam) meine Dame
mall *(AE)* [mɔːl] *überdachtes Einkaufszentrum*
mashed potatoes [mæʃt] Kartoffelbrei
memory ['memərɪ] Erinnerung
miracle ['mɪrəkl] Wunder
mist [mɪst] Nebel
misty ['mɪstɪ] nebelig
mood [muːd] Laune
motion ['məʊʃn] Bewegung
(to) **mow** [məʊ] mähen

N **needle** ['niːdl] Nadel
noon [nuːn] Mittag

O **old-fashioned** [əʊld'fæʃnd] altmodisch
onion ['ʌnjən] Zwiebel
organ ['ɔːgən] Orgel
ox, *pl.*: **oxen** [ɒks, 'ɒksən] Ochse

P **pajamas** *(AE)* = pyjamas *(BE)* [pə'dʒɑːməz]
paleface ['peɪlfeɪs] Bleichgesicht
pants (*pl.*) [pænts] *AE:* Hose
pep assembly *(AE)* ['pep ə'semblɪ] Anfeuerungsversammlung
performance [pə'fɔːməns] Vorführung
permit ['pɜːmɪt] Erlaubnis
(to) **persuade** [pə'sweɪd] überreden
physical therapist *(AE)* ['fɪzɪkl θerəpɪst] Krankengymnast/in
pickle ['pɪkl] saure Gurke
pie [paɪ] Kuchen
pillar ['pɪlə] Säule
pin-stripe ['pɪnstraɪp] Nadelstreifen
Pledge of Allegiance *(AE)* [pledʒ‿əv ə'liːdʒəns] Treueversprechen
(to) **plop** [plɒp] plumpsen
plum [plʌm] Pflaume
pom-pon *(AE)* ['pɒmpɒn] *großer „Bommel" z.B. aus Papierstreifen*
pork chop [pɔːk tʃɒp] Schweinekotelett
pouring [pɔːrɪŋ] strömend, giessend
prayer [preə] Gebet
(to) **press** [pres] drücken
profession [prə'feʃn] Beruf
prom [prɒm] *AE:* Schülerball
(to) **prove** [pruːv] beweisen
pumpkin ['pʌmpkɪn] Kürbis
puppy ['pʌpɪ] junger Hund, Welpe

R **raccoon** *(AE)* = racoon *(BE)* [rə'kuːn] Waschbär
raffle ['ræfl] Los
(to) **raise** [reɪz] aufziehen, anbauen
rather ['rɑːðə] lieber
recipe ['resɪpɪ] Rezept

refreshments *(pl.)* [rɪ'freʃmənts] Erfrischungen
refrigerator [rɪ'frɪdʒəreɪtə] Kühlschrank
rehearsal [rɪ'hɜːsl] Probe
reindeer ['reɪndɪə] Rentier
remind [rɪ'maɪnd] erinnern
reunion [riː'juːnjən] Treffen
rink [rɪŋk] Eisbahn
robe [rəʊb] Gewand; Bademantel
roller coaster ['rəʊlə kəʊstə] Achterbahn
row [rəʊ] Reihe

S **sale** [seɪl] Verkauf
salesman ['seɪlzmən] Verkäufer
salute [sə'luːt] Gruß
(to) **scare** [skeə] beängstigen
scary ['skeərɪ] ängstlich
scrambled eggs ['skræmbld] Rührei
service ['sɜːvɪs] Gottesdienst
(to) **shave** [ʃeɪv] rasieren
sheet [ʃiːt] Blatt
shooting star Sternschnuppe
shy [ʃaɪ] schüchtern
sidewalk *(AE)* Bürgersteig
(to) **sign up** ['saɪn ʌp] anmelden
(to) **skip** [skɪp] überspringen, auslassen
skunk [skʌŋk] Stinktier
sleigh [sleɪ] Schlitten
slim [slɪm] schlank
slope [sləʊp] Piste
smart [smɑːt] klug
snack [snæk] Imbiss
(to) **solve** [sɒlv] lösen
sophomore *(AE)* ['sɒfəmɔː] *Schüler/in der 10. Klasse*
speech [spiːtʃ] Rede
speedometer [spɪ'dɒmɪtə] Tachometer

spice [spaɪs] Gewürz
spicy ['spaɪsɪ] scharf gewürzt
(to) **spin** [spɪn] drehen
(to) **spread out** [spred] ausdehnen
stage [steɪdʒ] Bühne
stained-glass [steɪnd 'glɑːs] Buntglas
(to) **stampede** [stæm'piːd] stürmen
(to) **stare** [steə] starren
stepfather ['stepfɑːðə] Stiefvater
strapless ['stræplɪs] schulterfrei
stream [striːm] Strom
strife [straɪf] Unmut
string [strɪŋ] Saite
substitute ['sʌbstɪtjuːt] Vertretungslehrer/in
(to) **substitute** ['sʌbstɪtjuːt] vertreten
suit [suːt] Anzug
supper ['sʌpə] Abendessen
supposed to [sə'pəʊzd] sollen
Supreme Court *(AE)* [sʊ'priːm 'kɔːt] Oberster Gerichtshof

T **tassel** ['tæsl] Quaste, Troddel
taste [teɪst] Geschmack
(to) **tear** [teə] reißen
(to) **tip-toe** ['tɪptəʊ] auf Zehenspitzen gehen
tons of *(infml.)* ['tʌnz‿əv] sehr viele
tore → (to) **tear**
tough [tʌf] zäh
tournament ['tɔːnəmənt] Tournier
(to) **trace** [treɪs] verfolgen
trail [treɪl] Pfad; Weg
treat [triːt] kleine Überraschung, Freude
trim [trɪm] Verzierung
tuxedo *(AE)* [tʌk'siːdəʊ] Smoking
twinkling ['twɪŋklɪŋ] glitzernd

V **van** [væn] Kleinbus
(to) **vote** [vəʊt] wählen

W (to) **wallpaper** tapezieren
(to) **want sb. to do sth.** wollen, daß jd. etwas tut
(to) **wave** [weɪv] winken
well [wel] Bohrloch
(to) **whine** [waɪn] winseln
wide [waɪd] weit, groß
wig [wɪg] Perücke
witch [wɪtʃ] Hexe
(to) **work out** trainieren
(to) **wrap** [ræp] einpacken
wreath [riːθ] Kranz

Y (to) **yawn** [jɔːn] gähnen
(to) **yelp** [jelp] jaulen
YMCA (= Young Men's Christian Association) CVJM
yucky *(infml.)* ['jʌkɪ] unappetitlich